The Titus Ten

A W.I.N. Resource

Anita R Mckaney BSN

ISBN: 1492836664
ISBN 13: 9781492836667

Table of Contents

Dedicated to the Titus 2 women in my life:

Ruth Phelps
Gladys Harden
Great Aunt Mildred
My mom - Donita Harden

Preface

(Written in blog on May 13, 2013)

Words like discipline and discipleship have gotten my attention lately. I long to be Jesus's disciple and to disciple others. My spiritual gifts are varied. I have the gift of mercy, teaching and leadership. I find myself as a nurse instructor and lecturer today. Recently, the Lord has put it on my heart to teach more in the church. Now THAT is out of my comfort zone. However, I am the bondservant of the Lord so I will do as He asks. The Lord reminds me that I am already ministering online and in song (see www.tru-image.org or Tru Image and Tru Image Lifestyle Ministries on facebook). I have taught in front of groups of people before, but teaching the Word of God takes another level of faith. I feel the weight of responsibility to teach with integrity. The Lord had me going to nursing school, then put it to a halt momentarily and is sending me to evangelists and teachers who are mentoring me and training me to teach. Woah!

So, I am now in school online to learn how to teach the Word of God. The Lord reminded me that I prayed for instructors and mentors when he told me I would teach. Some interpret this gift as pastor-teacher, but I see it as two different gifts. The bible clearly says that the gifts of the Spirit are varieties and diversities of the operation and administration of gifts (I Corinthians 12:4-7). So there you have it! I also covet the gift of healing. O to have that spiritual gift! Anyway...I digress.

Discipleship is the goal for every christian. How can you say that you are growing in Christ when you still drink milk (Hebrews 5:12) and are not married (ie. committed to Christ (Luke 14:26-33) and multiplying (Matthew 28:19)? To go and teach is the same as making disciples. A disciple is a follower of God. However, my call is to make and to teach disciples to make disciples. God clearly told me to homeschool his children. I interpret that to mean that I am to teach those who are saved and those who will be saved. I am starting with my own children.

There is GREAT opposition to those who are disciple-makers. If the devil can steal the seed of the Word of God he has won a battle. He will, however, NEVER win the war! So, I am also learning to battle as a princess warrior in the Kingdom of God. Training is tedious. It basically involves forcing my flesh into submission to the Spirit so that God can use me 100%. I am studying the characters of the likes of Job, Daniel and Stephen. Again....not in the comfort zone. That is one way that I know I am in God's will. This is so NOT my idea!

Please pray for me men and women of the Most High. Pray that I will die daily to my flesh and clearly discern the voice of my Shepard (John 10: 16, 27). My goal is to walk by faith and not by sight.

Today, I rededicate my life to Jesus Christ. My life goal is to go and to teach all nations, baptizing them in the name of the Father, and of the Son, and of the Holy Ghost: teaching them to observe all things whatsoever He commands me. He will be with me always, even unto the end of the the world.

Introduction

The Lord has placed so many broken women before me. Some are hopeful for their marriages, others are hoping that divorce comes sooner than later. I have cried with women over the years and have had stern mothering moments with others. Over six years, my husband and I have been talking to people about marriage. My goal as a Wifestyle coach is to empower you to *do what you said* when you made your vows!

"....to have and to hold from this day forward for better or for worse, for richer for poorer,
in sickness and in health, to love and to cherish as long as we both shall live."

For Better or for Worse

For example, there is Candy (fictional name of course) - This wife has a well-kept secret. Her husband drinks and although he is not physically abusive, she is worried that he could be. It's been too emotionally taxing on her and she wants out of the relationship. There is no rebuttal from him about that at all, even when he's sober. My advice is not to divorce him but to pray to the Lord to reveal to her his source of hurt and that he is willing to get the assistance he needs to overcome this addiction. Prayer still works! If we truly believe that God is able to do exceedingly and abundantly above all that we can ask or think according to His riches in glory by Christ Jesus, we must pray like it! Life is not easy, especially if you are a wife. Your marriage is not to make all your dreams come true but to mold you into the image of Christ. This mold will press and force you to conform to God's mold for your life....if you are willing to be that is.

For Richer or Poorer

Victoria represents another wife that I have coached. She has abuse in her past and married Mr. Wrong in her opinion. The marriage started one way but is sadly veering in the other. Her hubby is literally "not who she married". He proclaims his love and faithfulness regularly, but is growing ever distant due to his pornography addiction that is draining the family funds dry. How can a wife be a "helper" in a situation like this? Tough love - that's how. Sometimes a man needs to hit rock bottom to bounce back. His mind needs to be renewed by the Great Physician. Sex is a powerful force in marriage and cannot be ignored. By taking the Word of God and applying it daily, it becomes a scalpel to sever soul ties and to repair the heart. A wife can help her husband by giving him time, space and leading him to the greatest Doctor of all time - Jesus!

In Sickness and In Health

Two couples come to my mind. The first is of a wife who could not bear her husband's illness. She left him. Sick. Alone. The marriage ended. In another relationship, Mary (alias) was sick herself and so was her husband. Instead of abandoning the relationship, she saw to it that he was cared for. In response, her husband did the same for her. It is hard to consider others before yourself especially if you don't think they are deserving. That is what a wife does who is walking in her calling. She looks like Jesus who laid down His life for all sinners.

Titus 2

In Titus, Paul tells the older women of the church to teach the younger. I hadn't considered myself an older woman until I realize that women younger than me were looking up to me. It's flattering, but it leaves me with an awesome sense of responsibility to assist these younger women to overcome the obstacles that I have overcome in my life and encouraging them to go even further than I have. Like Paul, I consider them like spiritual daughters. I have never had a daughter and so, I feel that this fills an incredible void in my life. You never know who is watching your life: your successes, failures, triumphal moments and biggest flops! But someone is. Someone ALWAYS is. I am at the age where I can see where I used to be and guide others, but I also am in need of my older sisters to guide me into older adulthood.

Once upon a time there was a wife. She was frustrated. She had a husband to care for and children to raise, a job to keep and a house to manage. It was overwhelming. She wondered if she was alone. She wondered if other women went through the same things as she did. She was busy. She was always busy doing something that she felt like God wanted her to do. But she was not focused. She was not doing whatever the one thing was that she could do best for the Lord. Then she decided to fast and ask the Lord what He wanted for her life. She came before God and told him that she would not move until He gave her specifics as to what to do. Wifestyle Image Network (W.I.N.) was then birthed in prayer and fasting.

Sometimes in life we overlook the simplest things. Even as a Christian who reads the Bible, nothing in it is truly understood until the Holy Spirit reveals it to you in a way that you can understand.

So why The Titus Ten? Titus - His name means "I Honor". He was a Gentile missionary. He was Paul's son in the faith and was discipled by him. He was a leader, a worker in the church, a speaker, exhorter and rebuker given authority by Paul. He was the first bishop of the Church of the Cretians. This is modern day Turkey. Their population was Jewish and Gentile. Paul was an apostle who planted the church. Titus was appointed the bishop. His job was to nominate overseers and elders of the churches there.

God showed me a vision of Titus 2 in action. In just an early morning time devotion, I received a revelation and quickly worked in obedience to the Holy Spirit. **There is just enough time to do exactly what God is calling you to do.** You may be wondering exactly what God is telling *you* to do. The answer lies in the Great Commission. In the book of Matthew, Jesus leave his disciples with a mission.

Then the eleven disciples went away into Galilee, into a mountain where Jesus had appointed them. And when they saw him, they worshipped him: but some doubted. And Jesus came and spake unto them, saying, All power is given unto me in heaven and in earth. Go ye therefore, and teach all nations, baptizing them in the name of the Father, and of the Son, and of the Holy Ghost: Teaching them to observe all things whatsoever I have commanded you: and, lo, I am with you always, even unto the end of the world. Amen. (Matthew 28:16-20).

The work of spreading the gospel and teaching others to do the same is hardly complete. There is still much work to be done. It is the *how to* that is the issue. If you are a born again believer then you already a great desire to share the Word of God with others. You may be ignoring it or you may not have clear direction as to where to start. If you are married then sharing the gospel may not even be among your highest of priorities. You may feel you are too old. You may feel you are too young. You may not have enough money and resources to spread the gospel. Your church may not have the right program in order for you to spread the gospel. Or, someone else can. Someone else has more experience more money that spiritual gift or calling, more training or a degree to do what God has called you to do.

Stop making excuses. I gave all those excuses to God (because they were mine as well) and He gave me His Holy Spirit to direct me in how to fulfill the mission He has clearly laid out. We only have so long to live and influence the world around us and then it is over. Jesus is coming back. He will want to know if the mission is complete or not. The bible speaks of seedtime and harvest time. The time to work for the Lord is now.

I must work the works of him that sent me, while it is day: the night cometh, when no man can work. (John 9:4)

Never before in the history of mankind have Christians all over the world been able to share the gospel so quickly and on such a massive scale. Never before have women in particular been able to have such a voice in other people's lives. Social media has become one of the primary means by which women of the 21st century communicate. It is through this vehicle that the Lord has blessed me to establish Wifestyle Image Networks across the globe. Wives network to establish mentoring relationships with younger women based on the ten Titus 2 directives given in scripture. Now that I know what to do and how to do it, I invite you, my readers from all over the world to join me on the greatest mission of all time!

It is by sharing the gospel, by shifting the focus from us to Christ, that people are drawn to God. Jesus said "And I, if I be lifted up, I will draw ALL men unto me". It's so not about you and I. It is admirable to look up to other leaders. The world has correctly interpreted and applied the concept of power in community. The more the merrier. It takes a village to raise a child. United we stand, divided we fall. However, when we only look to other people, mentors, parents or coaches as our sole source of confirmation, comfort or acknowledgement, we diminish the potential of God's power in our lives.

Where there is no counsel, the people perish; but in the multitude of counselors there is safety. - Proverbs 11:14

People will fail you. The bible is clear when it tells us to commit the gospel into the hands of faithful people who can commit it to other faithful people. It is free to all but only those who embrace and apply it are worth following. Hence the term disciple. This is more than a mere "come to the altar" experience. It is a long term relationship that focuses less and less on the discipler and more and more on Jesus who, in term will send the disciple out to disciple others. When the Lord finds that your growth is now sufficient for multiplication, he sends you to the field to be a seed that is broken but will yield more seed in that sacrifice.

Many have the right idea of small group growth but get uncomfortable with the idea of division but this, you see, is the goal. God never meant for us to be a small cluster of trees in unity. He envisions a forest that is thick and deep encompassing the earth. This is the Kingdom mindset versus ministry growth. God's plan is incomprehensible to the human mind that is why I have to use an analogy to even describe it.

The Lord is waiting to do exceedingly and abundantly above all that we can ask or think. He saves us, plants us, grows us, and then sends us to save, plant, grow and send out others. When we stay in one phase we are stagnant and not productive to the Kingdom.

Questions for Reflection
1. In an age when being old is unpopular, how does this commission for older women change your perspective?
2. What would being a mentor and a disciple look like in your life right now?
3. Jesus says we must count the costs of discipleship. How does following Him cost you?

Notes

Chapter 1

Submission

Whoever God loves he disciplines. He is the vine, we are the branches. If we are going to be true disciples, it is going to cost everything, not just the things you are willing to give up. I confess, for me it is a lot. For me discipleship looks like submission to my husband as the Lord revealed to me today. I was struck by the verse in 1st Peter that mentions Jesus willingness to be crucified on the cross and directly afterwards it says likewise likewise wives are to submit to their husbands. So God already knows that this is a difficult thing. He is already aware that it is not music to most women ears. But what are you really really willing to give up for Jesus?

I have been reading "Not a fan". I asked the Lord to prune me and to show me areas of my life where I have not completely surrendered to Him. This is one. I confess. It is hard to do. But the Word of God clearly says to submit to your husband as unto the Lord. If I am committed to follow Jesus Christ who is my Lord and he told me to follow my husband then it is only logical to be a submissive wife. Is it easy? No way! However if it is what my Lord commands, I will do it.

Please leave it in the comments for me the name of any disciple who had it easy. Please give me the scripture reference for any follower of Christ that was comfortable in their walk and did not have a thorn in the flesh or Satan on their tail.

In my opinion, marriage is a spiritual discipline all its own. There is no greater there has been no greater test of my face then my marriage. It is the most difficult thing for me to completely surrender to God because I have a great idea of what it should look like. My husband should love every idea I have and do things my way. Sound familiar? However, if I am to be a disciple it is not about my will, but God's will that must be accomplished in my life. So starting today, I am determined to live the life of discipleship starting with my marriage. Yes, I know I will be made fun of. Yes, I know that people will call me strange. However, if I looked just like everyone else and if I acted just like everyone else I would not be a disciple of Christ. If I do not hate my father mother sister and brother as Jesus says, how could I be his disciple?

Other people's opinions are insignificant to me at this point. Of course I will obey my husband IN the Lord and not OUT of the Lord's will. But how many times has he asked me to do something simple and I refused? God forgive me. I will repent which means that I will turn away from what I was doing and head in a different direction. Starting today. How about you?

Questions for Reflection
1. Would anyone describe you as a submissive person?
2. To what or to whom have you submitted yourself in the past?
3. Ask God how you can be completed submitted without reservation.

Notes

Chapter 2

Goodness

In Titus 2:5 older women are to teach younger women to be good. Goodness is a fruit of the spirit. The fruit of the spirit is actually one fruit (but that study is for another time). So, women need to be good, versus bad that is. The bible says that Jesus asked a question. "Why do you call me good? There is none good but God (Mark 10:18). He did not deny that He was good, for indeed He is, but His question was Why do you call Him that? It occurs to me that those described as good have some work or action done to be described that way. We often hear about the Good Samaritan. He was called good because he selflessly cared for another far beyond the reasonable expectation of so-called good people. His goodness is contrasted with the not-so-goodness of others. (Luke 10:25-37)

Luke 10:30-37 And Jesus answering said, A certain man went down from Jerusalem to Jericho, and fell among thieves, which stripped him of his raiment, and wounded him, and departed, leaving him half dead. And by chance there came down a certain priest that way: and when he saw him, he passed by on the other side. And likewise a Levite, when he was at the place, came and looked on him, and passed by on the other side. But a certain Samaritan, as he journeyed, came where he was: and when he saw him, he had compassion on him, And went to him, and bound up his wounds, pouring in oil and wine, and set him on his own beast, and brought him to an inn, and took care of him. And on the morrow when he departed, he took out two pence, and gave them to the host, and said unto him, Take care of him; and whatsoever thou spendest more, when I come again, I will repay thee. Which now of these three, thinkest thou, was neighbour unto him that fell among the thieves. And he said, He that shewed mercy on him. Then said Jesus unto him, Go, and do thou likewise.

Be good. We cannot understand goodness without knowing God. He is good. It is one of His many attributes. We cannot comprehend what is good without a comparison with something bad. The first use of the word good in the bible was the entrance of light into the darkness of earth. You see, the bible lets us know that earth was always dark - until God let there be light, which was good. So we see that goodness and light agree.

As a wife, our equivalent of goodness is being the light in dark places because light appearing from the darkness IS good! You may have heard it said that a woman is the thermostat of her home. She is the setter of the atmosphere and climate in her household.

We can also look at the story of Dorcas (Tabitha) in Acts 9:36-43. The bible says that she was full of good works and almsdeeds. She was like a modern-day fashion designer and taught other women to do the same. She was a disciple of Jesus Christ who took what she had and trained others to do the same. She modeled Jesus as she modeled her clothing. Let's take this a step further. In I Timothy 5:10 a disciple for Christ had to have a reputation for **good** work. For the wife, that means she is devoted to her tasks in and out of the home. We are to be rich in **good** works doing **good** according to I Timothy 6:18. Lastly, not only are we to work well but to show it to others in a discipling manner as Tabitha did.

I Timothy 2:9,10 In like manner also, that women adorn themselves in modest apparel, with shamefacedness and sobriety; not with broided hair, or gold, or pearls, or costly array; But (which becometh women professing godliness) with good works.

Sometimes, a woman is dressed so beautifully that everyone cannot help but to stop and stare. My goodness! Where did she get that dress? Who did her hair? Where did she get that bag? A wife dressed in good works will set the tone and change the atmosphere wherever she is! She shows up the darkness!

Want to see an atmosphere-changer in action? Look no further than Mary. not Jesus' mother, but the other Mary. This woman was the one who broke her Issey Miyake perfume bottle over Jesus' feet and wiped them with her hair. We see her at his feet again as he teaches while other women were doing "typical" womanly things. She was noticed for the **good** she did and Jesus commends her for the example she shows. Luke 10:42 says that Mary chose the **good** part!

Psalm 16:5-7 lets us know that we have a good heritage or inheritance when the Lord is our portion. Even in her death, Tabitha was seen as good. What good things will you be remembered for?

So we can take away three applications here. First, put on good works. They become who you are and how you are described. Secondly, Do good to others and it will teach those around you. Choose the good (Christ) because He is your inheritance. Your good for God is eternal and will never be overlooked. Exemplify and model goodness!

Questions for Reflection
1. Look at how many times goodness appears in the bible. Do a word study and journal your thoughts.
2. Goodness is a fruit of the Spirit. How can you further allow this fruit to develop in your life?
3. What would you like to be remembered for?

Notes

Chapter 3

Keepers at Home

This teaching is just what you think it is. Housekeeping, keeping the house. somebody has to work at home. We see the Proverbs 31 woman preparing food, fixing clothes and doing other household duties. She is not idle and we should not be either. Women of God must learn to be the administrators of the home. The up-keep of the house is a great responsibility and a privilege. I asked God about how to keep my home and three things emerged from that conversation. The physical atmosphere of the home is important. The emotional atmosphere of the home is equally important. The relationships within the home hold the house together or tear it apart.

The physical atmosphere speaks to cleanliness. In the Bible we see multiple examples of decency and order. God is a God of order. Is your house in order? When we go to a restaurant, you place an order expecting to be served. If the server owns the restaurant your service is best because their goal is to make you feel at home. They want you comfortable and to want to stay. That is how you want your home to feel to all who enter.

The emotional atmosphere is also important. Have you ever entered a home and the aura was disturbing, concerning or even frightening? Harmful words fill the atmosphere and you cannot sense the spirit of God in a home like that. Everyone there is hurt and wounded. It may feel like a prison or a psych ward. You just want out. Obviously, this is not God's plan. The wife sets the emotional temperature of her home. Even when it's tense, her reaction determines how the event plays out and how the atmosphere is "set".

Lastly, the relationships in the home determine if it is a house or a home. A man and a women with children define a household in biblical standards. Why does the Bible refer to keeping a house like you can lose it? I think it's because the whole idea of home and family is eroding in today's society. This is the key to the house. What is marriage and what is a family or a household was never in question before. Marriage refers to a covenant relationship between one man and one woman. A family consists of those who live together and are related by blood or are adopted into it. Being related by blood is important. Spouses are related by blood in a sexual union that can reproduce. God does not sanction unions that cannot reproduce. It is not in His nature to cease to multiply. It is not in God's plan to waste seed.

As we get closer to losing the meaning of family, we lose the home. It falls to the woman to be the keeper of the home. She makes sure that lost things (including the idea of home) get found. I remember when I was younger that it was always my mommy who found lost things. She had a place for everything and taught me how to put everything in its place. It's the same idea. Even passing on things like order and righteousness makes one a keeper of the home. She has the keys of the house. If they are lost, you lose the home.

When I was finally old enough to have my own set of house keys, it gave me a great sense of responsibility. I controlled who was in or out of the house. It is inherently implied through the Word of God that passing on the responsibility of household to your offspring is a woman's great pleasure as the Keeper of the Home. Like

God's Word, it's never just for you alone but for the generations that will follow after you. Teach those coming up behind you about the keys to the house unless you want strangers and thieves to steal what God has ordained in the home.

Questions for Reflection

1. Is your living space clean right now?

2. Keeping and managing a home is usually a wife's responsibility and privilege. What small steps can you take to maintain this gift from God?

Notes

Chapter 4

Chastity

G od has a blueprint - the Word of God. It tells us what the perfect building will look like. He gives this precious plan to us and as we construct our lives accordingly, but there will be setbacks and times when we try to alter His masterpiece. In the end, He will compare His plan for your life to what you have done with what He gave you.

Jeremiah 29:11 For I know the thoughts that I think toward you, saith the Lord, thoughts of peace, and not of evil, to give you an expected end.

Keeping yourself pure of sexual exploits for your spouse is a noble thing. Even if you have given away your virginity, or it was stolen from you, God can renew you for His purposes. God delights in making people new! He can still carry out the plan for your life!

II Corinthians 5:17 Therefore if any man be in Christ, he is a new creature: old things are passed away; behold, all things are become new.

Most of us know that maintaining virginity and celibacy equals purity when one is single, but what does it look like in marriage? The bible speaks of keeping the marriage bed pure. Pure physically, mentally and sexually. Any perversion or accessories to God's original blueprint are not what He is building. Remember, marriage is to represent Christ and His Church. He washes her. He covers her. He presents her without spot or wrinkle.

Ephesians 5:25-27 Husbands, love your wives, just as Christ also loved the church and gave Himself for her, that He might sanctify and cleanse her with the washing of water by the word, that He might present her to Himself a glorious church, not having spot or wrinkle or any such thing, but that she should be holy and without blemish.

I recently had a conversation with several women who shared their stories. We chatted about women addicted to porn and those with issues of masturbation in their marriages. This is hard. This is real. There should be nothing else needed or required by you to fulfill your sexual needs beyond the marriage bed with your husband. What happens in your bedroom is personal and private bringing other things and people within those sacred areas can prove to be a hinderance to what God has originally intended in the blueprint.

Sometimes the issues that affect a healthy sex life in marriage are hidden in our pasts. A vast majority of women have had some sexual encounter by their teen years that will resurface during marriage. This can affect your marriage later whether is it a disease history, promiscuity, rape, incest or abuse of any kind. This is why pre-marital counseling can be so helpful to women. In marriage, you dedicate your body to your spouse. It is only fair that you both know what has happened in the past so that you can move into the future without fear.

Here are Just a few testimonies from women I have spoken with recently.

Testimony #1
One woman had been abused by a man close to her and was already dealing with that pain when another man approached her sister. In an effort to protect her younger sister from rape, she offered herself instead out of desperation. Today she is married and tells others her story.

Testimony #2
Another woman lives with the memory of a rape that she hid because she was threatened. He told her that he would rape her sister if she told. However, today she is married to her Boaz, a caring man who treats her with dignity.

Testimony #3
Two women with sex issues prior to marriage have decided to combine their testimonies as a stepping stone into a ministry for other women.

No matter what has happened to you in the past, put God in control of your future. He alone can bring forgiveness, restoration and reconciliation in your relationship. If you are in need of counseling, I can do my best to put you in touch with a christian counselor in your area. Get the help you need to free yourself from bondage in any form and prepare for the calling that the Lord has already placed within you! He makes all things (even marriage) BETTER! You are His architect. Stick to the design.

Questions for Reflection
1. Surrender any past history to God that keeps you from seeing your-
self as chaste. Write out a prayer to God expressing our feelings.
2. What steps can you take to life a chaste lifestyle married or not? Make a plan and do it.

Notes

Chapter 5

Discretion

Discretion takes on many forms. Modesty is one of them, but even that is more than dress. It's attitude and apparel! It is defined as humility in character or not assuming so much about yourself. This wifestyle says "I must decrease. He (meaning Christ) must increase". Blessings should increasingly flow from your mouth, not cursing. What you wear should increasingly glorify God, not your body. This is what will set you apart from women in the world. Women of God who are waiting for a husband stand out in a crowd because she is modesty in her apparel and her attitude. A man of God will notice HER! The world has it so twisted. This is why christians are peculiar people and rightfully so!

Discretion also entails privacy. Some things about a woman should be quiet, secret, private. We learn this when we begin our menstrual cycles and start puberty. As you grow, you should also have a growing appreciation of the art of discretion. A lady knows when to speak and when not to, how to dress in various situations, how to hide and when to reveal. This is part of the essence of a Proverbs 31 woman. It really all comes down to timing. Ecclesiastes says that there is a time for everything under heaven! There is a time to cover up your body (singleness) and a time to reveal it (marriage). There is a time to be a student and a mentee and a time to be a teacher and a mentor. When we act outside of God's timing, we are not using discretion.

Being discreet is also using wisdom! Learning from others is a sure way not to repeat their mistakes. A wise woman watches, learns and only copies what works. Younger women often feel the need to correct their older predecessors, but wisdom tells us to observe and imitate. Men are captivated by a woman of discretion. How does she buy so many groceries for so little money? How does she keep the children in line so effortlessly? What makes her so impressive is her reliance on the Holy Spirit for moment-by-moment direction and her obedience.

The Holy Spirit is the hidden rudder that guides the massive ship of what I like to call Wifestyle. It is all in the "how". Being discreet is simply being submissive to the Holy Spirit before you are submissive to your husband. We must decide to be obedient before we are asked, to keep quiet and lay low until timing is impeccable. So next time you are about to make a decision, pause and ask God what the best way is to go about it. Inquire of an older woman and seek wisdom from the Word of God. This is discretion.

Questions for Reflection
1. In what ways have you NOT been discreet? How have you demonstrated discretion in other instances?
2. Look at women in the bible who practiced discretion (Esther, Abigail and Mary the mother of Jesus). How can you imitate them in your life?

Notes

Chapter 6

Love your Children

As a follower of Jesus Christ, we are also disciples. God calls us *apart* from the world and calls us *to* minister to others. We are all ministers of reconciliation as the Bible says in 2 Corinthians 5:18. Everyone that we come in contact with should encounter the love of Christ in some way. Have you thought about that? Whether it is in our own home, at work or in Walmart, we are living epistles to be read by all (2 Corinthians 3:2).

What does that look like at home? For the single person, it may mean weekend evenings that are booked serving in ministry at church instead of in the club. For the married among us, it may look like serving your spouse by doing chores or ministering to them physically. For the parent, it is seeing to it that your children have good Godly examples of Christ at work in a transformed life - yours!

In early church history, families were discipled, not just one person. A man or a woman would come to know Christ and then the family would follow. Our discipleship begins at home. Those closest to us should notice a change in our behavior, habits and desires. If this is not happening, perhaps we need to make sure of our conversion from darkness to light and ask the Lord to emblazon us with his fire. It is the Holy Spirit who convicts and allows fruit to develop in our lives. Let's all strive to be fruitful in our christian walk so that we can say "As for me and my house, we will serve the Lord!" (Joshua 24:15). One of my regular dilemmas is keeping my boys busy with wholesome, entertaining activity of substance. Sure they have the movies, tv, videos and modern things but they are Kingdom kids. To disciple them to be disciple-makers takes work!

Questions for Reflection
1. What steps can you take today to disciple your children?
2. If you have no children, how can you disciple other children?

Notes

Chapter 7

Love your Husband

So you may not know this about me, but I prefer to wear dresses and skirts most times. I am not necessarily convicted when I wear pants but I am free to chose. I chose to look and feel feminine, like a lady. I also notice that most men in my life (three in particular) prefer it too. I'm treated like a lady when I look, speak and act like one. It's true!

The same goes for my marriage. When I attempt to assert myself in a manly, authoritative manner I get nowhere. When I try to do manly things (fix my own car, play rough with my boys) I don't get far. I even get hurt! Now don't get me wrong. Women do many things and wear many hats, but being a married woman - you shouldn't have to. God instructs us to help not to tell our men to "get out of the way because I can do it better". However, many women are raised to dominate their men, to take control if you want it done right. You wear the pants, make the money, run the business and the vacuum.

We live in a single parent mindset society. Women certainly can do it all but God did not design us to. God did not tell you to be superwoman. He says that our role is to help. I ask God how to help and where to back off. We were not created to do it all. I let Maurice be the leader that he desires and was created to be. Why should your boss get more respect than your man? How come the things your hubby ask help with are still undone? If you are "the man of the house" your husband never will be.

You see, we are children of light. Women of God are supposed to be different, peculiar even, as compared to those who are conformed to the world's standards. If your wifely role at home blends into society's televised drama, I'm not surprised that your marriage is taking the hit. The bible emphasizes meekness for women. Meekness is not a doormat or a know-it-all. It is a character trait that displays gentleness, softness, submission and humility. That is what a woman with Tru-Image Wifestyle looks like. Wives were made to compliment their husbands masculinity. So let him wear the pants! Take a deep breath. Relax and prioritize then work your wifestyle!

Lately, I have been talking to God about my marriage. I want it to be even better than what it already is! Since we are in ministry together, people are often asking us questions and want our viewpoint on various topics. I get asked about sex, money, kids, divorce, porn, abuse, you name it. So, it makes me want my own marriage in tip top shape!

My marriage legacy will be left to my two sons. What they see, hear and learn, whether spoken or unspoken, will influence the next generation. I pray that they want a wife who is good to them "like mommy is to daddy".

I want them to see Christ and His Church. I want them to see a man and woman in love - the mushy gushy kind and the "I would die for you" kind. I want them to say that their parents laughed so hard together and that they embraced each other through the hard times. I want every sacrifice in my marriage to scream "I love you this much".

My desire is to walk together towards God with my husband. That was the theme of our wedding. We will be so close that no person, place or thing can divide us. We will be so focused that even though the road is narrow, by instinct, we make room for each other. We will be so attracted to the things of God that even though in heaven there will be no husbands and wives, we will be more delighted to be One with our Creator forever.

Questions for Reflection
1. Whether married or not, you should be preparing to be a bride.
How are you preparing to serve your Husband?
2. How do you display love to your husband? Read I Corinthians 13 and put your name in every place where you see Love or Charity. Is it still a true scripture? How can you make it true?

Notes

Chapter 8

Thirsty

What are you thirsty for? Drinking does not satisfy your thirst, Christ does. He is the living water. What are you addicted to? When you are drunk or full of alcohol, you are oblivious to things that you paid attention to before. You may even notice things that are not there. Your sensitivity changes and your reaction time is not as sharp. The bible speaks of Hannah who in her desperation pleaded before the Lord in prayer for a child. The priest in the temple thought she was drunk. Her lips were moving but he heard no sound. In Acts 2, we see the Holy Spirit descend on the apostles who spoke with new tongues and everyone heard them in their own language. The sense of hearing affects how you react to the reality of a situation. I had never noticed much before that it was the hearing of the mighty rushing wind filling the house that caused a change in the sense of hearing. It's all about how you hear! Hannah was assumed to be drunk and in sin, whereas the disciples were interpreted by men from all over the globe who could hear them speak in their language.

This has several implications for us. First of all, who are you listening to. They don't call alcoholic drinks spirits for no reason. Drunks act uncharacteristically because it is the spirit controlling them. When we allow ourselves to be full of the Holy Spirit, we act and react more like Christ. It's not in our nature, it's supernatural.

Secondly, some people will consider you strange and peculiar (like a typical lush) when you are changed by the Spirit of God. Suddenly you don't fit in anymore. They can pick you out of the crowd because your "slurred speech" betrays you as not being from around here. Have you ever been able to detect a foreigner's place of residence by their accent. Yeah, it's like that.

When you serve God and He fills you with His Spirit, there is no denying it. Hannah adamantly refused the fact that she was drunk and the Lord sent a witness with the apostles who made it clear that they were not drunk either. Are you identified with Christ by being seen drunk in the club? Or are people curious about you because you stand out from the crowd? One thing about thirsty folks is, they always want more. What are you thirsty for, the next drink or the very presence of God?

Questions for Reflection

1. Would you say that you have had a personal experience with the Holy Spirit? If not, ask God to fill you. If so, would you say that you are being re-filled regulary?
2. Drinking dulls the senses. How can we be sensitive to the Spirit instead?

Notes

Chapter 9

Gossip

Did you hear what she said about you? Tell me what happened. Who did what? Gossiping is not becoming of a woman of faith. Gossips are tellers of tales, a betrayer of confidences and teller of secrets. The Bible says much especially to women about watching our mouths and tongues.

And the tongue is a fire, a world of iniquity: so is the tongue among our members, that it defileth the whole body, and setteth on fire the course of nature; and it is set on fire of hell. (James 3:6).

A talebearer revealeth secrets: but he that is of a faithful spirit concealeth the matter. (Proverbs 11:13)

Why is gossip such a big deal? It is for several reasons. It makes you untrustworthy. It hurts other people and their reputations through slander and It is is not a good use of your tongue or time. Gossip is a serious sin.

And even as they did not like to retain God in their knowledge, God gave them over to a reprobate mind, to do those things which are not convenient; Being filled with all unrighteousness, fornication, wickedness, covetousness, maliciousness; full of envy, murder, debate, deceit, malignity; whisperers, Backbiters, haters of God, despiteful, proud, boasters, inventors of evil things, disobedient to parents, Without understanding, covenant-breakers, without natural affection, implacable, unmerciful: Who knowing the judgment of God, that they which commit such things are worthy of death, not only do the same, but have pleasure in them that do them. (Romans 1:28-32)

I'm sure you have been around other women who always have something to say or something to tell about someone. We are so like the serpent in the Garden of Eden when we gossip! Did God really say this or that? Lying, deception and gossip are friends that stick closely together. A woman of God must use discernment with her speech and not keep company with others who have no control over theirs.

Do a friend inventory (on and off social media). What are your friends talking about? It is edifying or building up another person. Is it fruitful and encouraging or is everything you see on facebook, twitter, instagram and KIK demeaning, insulting or simply unnecessary? The Lord is not a waster of time or words. You are on this earth with a mission. You are an ambassador for Christ and a soldier on the battlefield for lost souls in need of salvation.

"Therefore if any man be in Christ, he is a new creature: old things are passed away; behold, all things are become new. And all things are of God, who hath reconciled us to himself by Jesus Christ, and hath given to us the ministry of reconciliation; To wit, that God was in Christ, reconciling the world unto himself, not imputing their trespasses unto them; and hath committed unto us the word of reconciliation. Now then we are ambassadors for Christ.." (2 Corinthians 5: 17-20).

No man that warreth entangleth himself with the affairs of this life; that he may please him who hath chosen him to be a soldier (2 Timothy 2:4).

Perhaps, you are unsure of your mission or even your reason for living. Dedicating your tongue and your life to Christ is simple. Admit that you have sinned and done wrong and that Jesus Christ died for your sins on the cross of Calvary. We have all sinned and not met God's standards of right living. Don't beat yourself up about it, give all your sin to Jesus. Believe that He took care of all of them on the cross and that He died but rose again from the grave to triumph over death for you. Believe that he exchanges your sin or eternal life and that it is a free gift for everyone willing to receive it. Confess with your mouth that you are now in the family of God and get baptized so that your faith is made public. Baptism symbolizes the death of the old you and a fresh, clean beginning including the use of your tongue. Welcome to the family of God sis!

Questions for Reflection
1. What are some ways that you can avoid gossip?
2. Replacing gossip begins with how you think. How can you change
your mindset to line up with the Word of God?
3. Have you been baptized? If not, make plans to obey the Lord in this.

Notes

Chapter 10

Holiness

When something is Holy, that means that it is set apart, dedicated and consecrated for a specific purpose and use. When God formed woman from man, she was a new creation made by a loving God just for His purposes. You are especially designed by the Master as a jewel for His glory and His pleasure. No matter what you think of yourself, you are a Princess in the most royal of Royal Courts. You belong to the family of the King of Kings and not only that, but you are chosen as His bride to reign by His side forever. When you embrace who you are dear sister, you life should line up accordingly. When was the last time you saw someone of the Royal family in want for anything or mingling with the commoners? It doesn't happen. You stand out from the crowd because of your Godly heritage, the angelic hosts are your bodyguards and you have no want at all. Ever. You are held to a higher standard of holiness because of your position and status in the Kingdom. You life should not look "normal". The church is called a "peculiar people" in the bible.

"But ye are a chosen generation, a royal priesthood, an holy nation, a peculiar people; that ye should shew forth the praises of him who hath called you out of darkness into his marvellous light.." (I Peter 2:9).

Sister, you are the bride of Christ. The church is referred to in the feminine in the Word of God. The bible says that His church is dressed in white, which stands for purity and holiness. You are set apart from the world for God's own glory. He is your husband and Lord. God's children are clothed as a bride (Isaiah 49:16-18). We should be devoted to God as a bride is to her husband (Jeremiah 2:1-3). The church is the bride of Christ set apart in holiness to Him. (2 Corinthians 11: 1,2). The righteous Bride of Christ will be presented to Christ in heaven when all His enemies are defeated. (Revelation 19: 6-9).

"Sing, O barren, thou that didst not bear; break forth into singing, and cry aloud, thou that didst not travail with child: for more are the children of the desolate than the children of the married wife, saith the LORD. Enlarge the place of thy tent, and let them stretch forth the curtains of thine habitations: spare not, lengthen thy cords, and strengthen thy stakes; For thou shalt break forth on the right hand and on the left; and thy seed shall inherit the Gentiles, and make the desolate cities to be inhabited. Fear not; for thou shalt not be ashamed: neither be thou confounded; for thou shalt not be put to shame: for thou shalt forget the shame of thy youth, and shalt not remember the reproach of thy widowhood any more. For thy Maker is thine husband; the LORD of hosts is his name; and thy Redeemer the Holy One of Israel; The God of the whole earth shall he be called. For the LORD hath called thee as a woman forsaken and grieved in spirit, and a wife of youth, when thou wast refused, saith thy God. For a small moment have I forsaken thee; but with great mercies will I gather thee. In a little wrath I hid my face from thee for a moment; but with everlasting kindness will I have mercy on thee, saith the Lᴏʀᴅ thy Redeemer. (Isaiah 54:1-8)

Jesus has washed, cleaned and beautified you with salvation, so hold your head up high beautiful one. Although used, abused and cast aside by the enemy of your soul sister, You are His pretty woman. The world is watching and waiting for the marriage Supper of the Lamb and the Church is His Holy Bride.

Questions for Reflection
1. Do you have issues with being "peculiar"? How do you see yourself in light of God's Word now?
2. Being the Bride of Christ is a privilege. How does this knowledge change
your perspective? What will you do with this information?

Notes